The rise o

BY
roLanD L

STOCKTON

TO

maLone!

Published by Addax Publishing Group
Copyright © 1998 by Roland Lazenby
Designed by Anonymouse Graphics
Cover Design by Jerry Hirt
Photos by Bill Smith
Cover photo by Don Grayston

For information address:
Addax Publishing Group
8643 Hauser Drive, Suite 235, Lenexa, KS 66215

ISBN: 1-886110-43-3

Distributed to the trade by Andrews McMeel Publishing
4520 Main Street
Kansas City, MO 64111

Printed in the United States of America
1 3 5 7 9 10 8 6 4 2

This book is not an official publication of, nor is it endorsed by,
the Utah Jazz.

Library of Congress Cataloging-in-Publication Data

Lazenby, Roland.
        Stockton to Malone : the rise of the Utah Jazz / by Roland
    Lazenby.
            p. cm.
        ISBN 1-886110-43-3
        1. Utah Jazz (Basketball team)--History. 2. Stockton, John, 1962-
        3. Malone, Karl. I. Title.
        GV885.52.U8L39   1998
        796.323'64'09792258--dc21   98-6540
                                                                CIP

Contents

Introduction

This is a story of the uncompromising competitiveness of three men—Utah Jazz power forward Karl Malone, point guard John Stockton and coach Jerry Sloan.

For the past decade, Sloan has been the hard-nosed officer in charge of the Jazz, a voice from the old school demanding the ultimate competitive effort from his players. Stockton and Malone are the on-court charges who execute Sloan's vision. They are the premier point guard and power forward of their time, yet they are as decidedly old school in their approach as Sloan himself. They turn their noses up at the empty flattery of stardom and focus on one thing, their quest of many seasons to win the NBA title. It is this approach that has given the Utah Jazz a remarkable team chemistry, that makes the team's stars unique in modern professional athletics.

"They're superstars who are down home," says 13-year veteran Antoine Carr, who came to Utah just before the 1994-95 season, of Malone and Stockton. "I mean, I've run across a lot of guys in this league who thought they were better than everybody else and kind of carried themselves that way. But these guys are normal guys. They like to go fishing, hunting. They hang out together, do those things together. I've never really seen superstars like that."

Adam Keefe, who came to Utah in a September 1994 trade from Atlanta, said he was surprised when his new superstar teammates phoned to see if he needed help moving in. "The first thing that struck me," Keefe says, "is the type of people they are. They're completely unpretentious. They both do such a great job of keeping their lives in perspective."

The atmosphere that Stockton and Malone set around the Jazz makes it easier for the lesser players to find their confidence, Keefe says. "The important thing about their leadership is that they're not spokesmen; they're not flamboyant characters. They lead by their actions on the court, by demonstrating through their intensity and work ethic.

"Neither one of them will ever be late for a bus, a practice or a

Karl Malone is one of pro basketball's all-time greatest

game. Neither one of them will ever cut corners in practice. In that sense they never take advantage of the special position they're in, and that's what makes them so tremendous."

This stands in stark contrast to Keefe's experience in Atlanta, playing alongside Dominique Wilkins. "For me, especially, what a difference, coming from where I came from," he says. "Here, they appreciate and understand the small things that get done. Karl's great. If you set a pick for him to get him open, he'll say, 'Thanks.'

"They understand what it takes, that it's not the world revolving around them on the basketball court, that they need other compo-

nents out there. They're both phenomenal in that sense. They're not concerned with how they're seen in the big picture, if they drive the nicest cars or have the most flamboyant clothing. That doesn't appeal to them. What appeals to them are the basics of life—and winning."

Malone says he likes to think of a quote he read by Dallas Cowboys quarterback Troy Aikman about how it's important to walk with your teammates, not out in front of them. "Everybody talks about the superstar status," Malone says. "I don't know how they're supposed to act. That's not how I was brought up. If we were horses' behinds, there'd be total chaos in this locker room.

"It's great when the coach calls your play, and you make a pass to your teammate. That's your play, and you can do anything you want with it. All of a sudden, your teammates say, 'I feel a part of

this.' And that's what it's all about. It's not about me, me, me. It's about us, and that's the only way I know how to be."

And that is why, to a man, the Jazz are focused on a single goal. "If you watch the way we play," Antoine Carr says, "the guys are all high-fiving from one to 12. That's something special. You don't get that very often.

"We're gonna try," Carr says, "as hard as we can to do what Karl wants to do and what John wants to do, which is win the championship."

What follows is the story of Stockton, Malone, Sloan and company's uncommon effort to reach a common goal.

STOCKTON TO MALONE

The scenes repeat themselves almost every night.

The Utah Jazz badger an opponent into taking a bad shot, and instantly Karl Malone releases upcourt. Underneath, Jazz center Greg Ostertag grabs the defensive rebound and contemplates for a fraction of a second what to do with it. John Stockton rushes up to demand the ball. Ostertag gives it up, and Stockton immediately hurls it the length of the floor, where it falls into Malone's waiting hands just two steps from the hoop for the easy layup.

Ker-ching. Stockton and Malone ring up another two points, another assist. It is an act they have executed thousands of times over the past dozen seasons playing together. How perfectly numerical it is that as Stockton, the National Basketball Association's all-time leader in assists and steals, closes in on 13,000 assists, Malone will be busy logging his 27,000th point.

Moments later, the Jazz are running their half court offense. Malone sets the pick high and rolls to the left side of the lane. The slightest crease of a passing lane opens, and Malone turns his massive 6-9, 256-pound body just enough to pin the defender on his hip. Stockton threads the bounce pass low and away, so that only Malone can reach it. He scoops it up like gravy and pivots, executing a sweet drop step. Ker-ching. Another easy layup. Another assist.

Then there's Stockton on the break, moving full speed, with his head turning like a swivel, surveying the options, seeing who's with him on the wings. Stockton keeps pushing and penetrates, and then does what every coach tells a point guard not to do: He leaves his

feet. In mid-air, he looks hard right to the deep corner where Jazz forward Bryon Russell awaits the pass. But at the last instant, Stockton flips the ball back over his left shoulder, across the key to where Malone has spotted up for an open jumper. Ker-ching.

"Stockton and Malone operate like they're on one wavelength," says Jazz broadcaster Hot Rod Hundley, who has spent the past decade watching Utah's special combination. "Basketball requires split-second timing. They have a relationship no one else can fill. I've watched this game all my life and played against the best players and seen the best, and I've never seen two players play as well together as those two. The way they look at each other. They know each other's every move. It's a matter of a split second, whether you succeed or not. In particular, the pick and roll has to be perfect. And no one does it better than those two."

"There's a comfort level with Karl," the 36-year-old Stockton explains. "He's got great hands. There doesn't have to be that big of a gap to get him the ball. He can catch it. He can get himself in position. With that, there's a lot of confidence in the passes you throw him."

Confidence, indeed. Stockton led the NBA in assists for an unprecedented nine straight seasons, until the 1996-97 campaign when he relinquished the crown to Mark Jackson and finished second. The much-revered Oscar Robertson led the league six times, but never more than three seasons in a row.

Stockton also holds the record for assists in a season (1,164 in 1990-91). Only 10 times in league history has a player totalled more than 1,000 assists. Eight of those seasons belong to Stockton.

Conversely, Malone has racked up 10 consecutive seasons of 2,000 or more points scored (by comparison, Wilt Chamberlain only produced seven such seasons), which leads to the inevitable questions about who is more responsible for this success, Stockton or the 35-year-old Malone?

The answer, of course, is that they both share the glory as the sole members of an intensely competitive, exclusive club. "I don't know if two players will ever come together on the same team with the same kind of talent and the same motivation," says Jerry Sloan, the man who has coached them for nine seasons. "It is unique."

DRAFT-DAY STEALS

Their story is all the more special once you consider the fact that these guys didn't earn scholarships to big-time colleges and weren't selected as lottery picks in the NBA draft. Malone, who went to Louisiana Tech, was taken by the Jazz with the 13th selection of the first round of the 1985 draft.

The eighth of nine children, Malone was raised in the little town of Summerfield, Louisiana, where in the seventh grade he took up basketball. Within three seasons he had become quite proficient at the game, leading his Summerfield High team to the first of three consecutive state titles.

Those championship performances and a growth spurt that pushed him to 6-9 by his senior season were enough to warrant All-America recognition and a scholarship offer from nearby Louisiana Tech, where his presence would loom so large that it would prompt *Shreveport Times* reporter Teddy Allen to nickname Malone "the Mailman" because of his knack for delivering in big games.

Stockton, who played college ball at Gonzaga in Spokane, Washington, near the neighborhood tavern that his parents own and operate, was taken by the Jazz with the 16th overall pick in 1984. "John never started out as the best player in his age group," his father Jack recalled a few years back. "But he was always gaining on everybody. And there were some tremendous matches with the older boys. That's when I started seeing it coming. John never got beat the same way twice. They'd pop around him pretty good. But the next day they'd have to find another way to beat him."

That competitiveness drove Stockton to success at Gonzaga Prep and to the top of Spokane-area All-Star teams, then on to a stellar college career at Gonzaga, where his grandfather earned All-America distinction in 1924 as a triple-threat running back.

There were immediate doubters when the Jazz used a first-round pick to get Stockton in 1984, but the team's circumstances allowed him to find success. Playing as a backup, as a rookie, he appeared in all 82 games in 1984-85 and averaged 5.6 points.

"I played behind a great player in Rickey Green [when I was] coming into the league," Stockton says. "I was afforded the chance to just play and not have to help a team get better. Rickey was so good and everybody relied so heavily on him. When I was in, I was in to try to play well. I guess I didn't have any of that added pressure."

"Playing well" became his trademark. What amazes Sloan 13 seasons later is that Stockton has continued to perform at a very high level, despite the fact that he's supposedly well past his prime.

In fact, Sloan says he can't think of undersized player who remained on top of the game at age 36. "Not at that size," Sloan said of the 6-1, 175-pound Stockton. "I've seen a lot of big guys who can play pretty well. But not that size. You don't find point guards that size who still exist in the league, let alone play effectively. I've never seen too many of 'em or don't know of too many of 'em. But John's got tremendous pride. He takes tremendous care of himself."

Malone shows just the same care and is fanatical about his off-season training regimen. When the Denver Nuggets coaches were in Salt Lake City over the summer of 1997 to prepare for a rookie summer league game, they were stunned to encounter Malone early one July Sunday morning working alone in a local health club. New Nuggets coach Bill Hanzlik was so excited by the sight of Malone sweating through an intense lifting workout, that he went across the street to his hotel and awakened his rookies. He then had them come over to the health club to watch a champion at work.

"I'd always heard that Karl was one of the best-conditioned athletes in the game," Nuggets rookie Bobby Jackson told Mike Monroe of the *Denver Post*. "Now I know why. He wants to win and he knows what it takes. I just have a lot of respect for him. There are only a few guys who work the way he does."

"What a great experience," agreed Nuggets rookie Danny Fortson. "I was amazed to see all the stuff Karl does. . . I mean he's a legend. To see how hard he works, even in summer, it makes you want to learn from him and work just as hard as he does."

Sloan says that work ethic has meant that each and every season Stockton and Malone have come into camp in impeccable shape. "I've been very lucky," Sloan says. "I don't think anybody in the coaching business could be more fortunate than I am, to have two guys like that."

Which helps explain why they each had missed a total of only four games over the first 12 grueling campaigns of their careers.

It also helps explain how Stockton, after suffering a serious knee injury during the 1997 preseason, was able to undergo rehab and rejoin the team by December. He missed the season's first 18 games, which brought to an end his streak of 609 consecutive games played. There was quiet talk that the injury probably meant the end of his career, but Stockton paid attention to none of that.

"Once the decision was made to have the surgery, I was resigned to the fact that I was going to miss some games," Stockton said of his injury. "It wasn't fun. But, at that point, I looked beyond the facts that I was going to miss games and how many I was going to miss, and focused on trying to do the things that would get me back quicker. Things that [would] have me in as good of a condition I could be in, so when the surgery healed well enough, I would already be in good enough shape to start playing."

Within weeks after his return, it was obvious that Stockton was back in peak form. "Injuries can create a little doubt in your

mind," Malone said after watching Stockton's return in December 1997. "But he's the kind of guy who really knows how to work to get back. He's definitely back to where he was."

NUMBERS

Despite the fact that they relentlessly continue to stack up superior numbers in points and assists, both Stockton and Malone hate talking about them.

You can hear the disdain in Stockton's voice at their mere mention. You talk numbers, he sneers. In January and February 1995, as he closed in on the NBA's all-time assist mark held by Magic Johnson, he gave media questioners the same pat response when asked about his milestone.

"It's just a stat," he said. "It's not winning and it's not losing."

Malone holds a similar view of his individual achievements. "I'm in this thing for one reason," he says, "and that's to win it."

They're right, of course. Numbers are for losers and also-rans. Numbers are a salve for people who don't win championships. Stockton and Malone don't want a salve.

As Stockton steadily moved up the all-time assist standings in 1995, passing Bob Cousy, Isiah Thomas, Oscar Robertson and finally Magic, reporters would ask him what it was like to join their special company. "I don't know if it puts me in their company or not," he would reply. "Those guys are all something special."

What he meant is that Cousy, Robertson, Thomas and Johnson all played on at least one championship team. For all of their numbers, Stockton and Malone don't have the only validation that truly matters.

In the 1992 Olympics, when Stockton played with Johnson on Dream Team I, the Utah playmaker had only one question for the great Laker floor leader: "How did you win all those champi- onships?"

Discovering the answer to that riddle is a quest that drives Stockton, Malone and Sloan, an intensely competitive trio who share a passion for a spare, hard-driving brand of basketball stripped of the nonsense that seems to permeate the modern NBA.

For years they've operated by Sloan's simple, uncompromising code: You compete relentlessly, and you have no fear of facing the consequences.

"Just hope your players come and play as hard as they can," Sloan says. "That's all you can ask. If they play as hard as they can, they walk off the floor and they know they've done their best. If you lose, fine. If you win, fine. Go home."

It's an approach that has kept them battling against the odds season after season without giving in to the frustrations that have sidetracked other teams and other players. "I've always thought our teams have had pride, our players have had pride," Sloan says. "We've experienced a lot of failures over the years. But it takes a lot of pride. You have to have a lot of pride in yourself to keep coming back and trying."

FIRST THE BLUES

When it comes to basketball heartaches, the Jazz have certainly had their share. They were born in the city of jazz, New Orleans, in 1974, and promptly did a decade of penance in the dank basement of the NBA, facing the misery of losing season after season.

Fortunately, the agony wasn't without moments of relief. Early in their existence, the Jazz traded with the Atlanta Hawks to get the immensely entertaining Pistol Pete Maravich. Today, Stockton operates with the cold precision of a brilliant surgeon, firing laserlike passes just where they ought to be and thrilling fans and teammates with a superior competitive logic. Maravich, on the other hand, usually approached the basketball from one of two

*The addition of Jeff Hornacek gave Utah a
dependable third scoring option.*

perspectives, either behind the back or between the legs. With his floppy socks and long hair, he ran the franchise's first team like an improvisational band leader. They were, after all, the Jazz.

And they were often fun to watch. They just didn't win much. In fact, they lost 13 of the first 14 games in team history and promptly fired their first coach, Scotty Robertson. Butch van Breda Kolff replaced him and steered the club to a 5-42 record through Janaury, when magically they got in tune.

The Jazz ran off an 18-17 record down the stretch to finish the 1974-75 season with a 23-59 record, respectable for an expansion franchise. The next season they bumped the numbers to 38-44, and Maravich averaged 25.9 points, third highest in the league, and gained a berth on the All-NBA Team. His game was showmanship at its purest, and for the 1976-77 season his scoring numbers jumped to 31.1 points per game, tops in the league. With the record at 14-12, the Jazz abruptly switched coaches, dismissing van Breda Kolff and promoting assistant Elgin Baylor, a change that produced only a 35-47 finish.

The franchise slipped deeper into doom that season with an ill-fated trade package that would bring 11-year veteran guard Gail Goodrich from the Lakers for a pair of draft picks, one of which would be used by Los Angeles to select Magic Johnson in 1979. Goodrich, meanwhile, was well past his prime, and the deal left Lakers management snickering.

That February of '77 Maravich scored 68 points against the New York Knicks, the pinnacle of his individual brilliance. Eleven months later he would injure his knee while attempting a between-the-legs pass, and his star would never shine quite so brightly again.

The franchise added to its offbeat image that spring of '77 by becoming the first NBA team to draft a woman, Lucy Harris, who did not make the roster. However, Jazz fans did get their first view of a real power forward that fall with the appearance of Leonard "Truck" Robinson, a 6-7, 225-pounder who had seven 20-

Pistol Pete was the band leader in the early days.

rebound games in a two-month period. The effort helped him gain All-NBA honors and moved the club closer to .500 with a 39-43 finish.

New Orleans, though, struggled through 1978-79 with a 26-56 record, the worst in the NBA, the product of yet another terrible deal: trading Truck Robinson to Phoenix for guard Ron Lee, forward Marty Byrnes, two first-round draft picks, and cash.

With the club's prospects sinking, co-owners Sam Battistone and Larry Hatfield elected to abandon the Big Easy and its raucous spirit for the quieter big scenery of Utah. The wisdom of such a dramatic shift was immediately challenged by observers around the league, but Utah was a state with a deep interest in hoops that grew from the grass roots of the Mormon faith. Besides, the American Basketball Association's Utah Stars had enjoyed some success in attracting fans and had even managed to win the 1971 ABA title under coach Bill Sharman. The franchise had closed shop after the 1975 season as the ABA melted away, but the hunger for pro basketball was still alive in Salt Lake City.

A month after announcing the move, the owners named Frank Layden, an overweight former assistant coach with the Atlanta Hawks, as the team's general manager. He had a good eye for talent to go with his big appetite, and his sense of humor was pure Brooklyn. Among his best first moves, was the trading of Spencer Haywood to the Lakers for a young 6-5 forward named Adrian Dantley. The trade didn't exactly make up for the Gail Goodrich deal, but it helped as Dantley averaged 28 points per game for 1979-80. The Jazz as a whole averaged 102.4 points per game, last in the league, a stat that gives the reader an idea just how far offenses in the NBA have slipped in recent seasons. Today, those numbers would rank at the top of the league.

With Tom Nissalke replacing Baylor as coach, the club posted a 24-58 record, yet the Jazz were still good enough to attract an occasional sell-out in the Salt Palace (capacity 12,015).

The poor finish meant that in the 1980 draft Layden could take the college player of the year, Darrell Griffith, a 6-4 guard from the University of Louisville. It didn't hurt that he was nicknamed "Dr. Dunkenstein" and had a perimeter game to go with his ability to get to the rim. His presence, though, couldn't save the Jazz from another season of misery. That January of '81, as the team was on its way to a 54-loss season, Layden released Maravich, who had continued to struggle in his return from knee injuries.

Layden named himself head coach after the club again got off to a pitiful start in 1981, which set in motion the chain of events that would eventually bring together the Stockton to Malone combination.

As the core of the young Jazz, Griffith and Dantley churned through yet another desperate campaign, again failing to win 30 games. The low point perhaps came in 1982-83, when Dantley missed 60 games with a wrist injury and the club again finished in misery, with just 30 wins. Each year's draft, though, was bringing more talent. Shot-blocking center Mark Eaton, a lightly-regarded prospect out of UCLA, came in the fourth round in 1982 (Dominique Wilkins was the first rounder that year but was promptly traded to Atlanta in a package that brought talented but troubled John Drew, who immediately went into drug rehab for eight weeks).

Forward Thurl Bailey arrived in the '83 draft with guard Bobby Hansen. Despite his marginal coaching records, Layden survived a change of ownership that offseason, as Dr. Gerald Bagley and his son acquired controlling interest in the team.

The breakthrough for Layden began that fall of 1983, as the Jazz, with the core group of Dantley, Griffith, Eaton, Thurl Bailey and Rickey Green, started with a big offensive blast (they would average 115 points per game). By the All-Star break, they had the best record in the Western Conference on their way to a 45-37 finish, the Midwest Division title, and their first playoff appearance, highlighted by beating the Denver Nuggets in the first round of the playoffs before falling to Phoenix in the second. The effervescent

Hornacek helps Stockton handle the pressure.

Layden was named NBA coach of the year, and after nine straight losing seasons, the franchise had a new and improved self-concept.

Little did anyone suspect that when Layden picked Stockton in the first round that spring of 1984, the team had just acquired the bedrock of its future, or at least half of it. Layden would add the other half the following spring with the selection of Malone.

On the verge of great success, the Jazz instead had to deal with the trappings of prosperity. Dantley held out, seeking more money, and Drew caved in to his personal demons, drawing a suspension. Despite the distractions, the club struggled along to a 41-41 record. With each game, it became increasingly apparent that Eaton could play a major role in the pro game. At season's end, the 7-4 center, who had set all-time league records for total blocks (456) and blocks per game (5.56), was named the league's defensive player of the year.

In the playoffs, the Jazz took the Houston Rockets in five games, but Eaton was injured and the club promptly lost four straight to the Denver Nuggets in the second round.

The next big burst of momentum came that spring when Larry Miller, the owner of a network of 30 auto dealerships across the Southwest, purchased a 50% interest in the franchise from Sam Battistone. A former fast pitch softball player of some merit, Miller brought business acumen, community stability and competitive focus to the team, setting in motion the next stage of growth. The frustrations, however, didn't disappear immediately.

The ups and downs continued from there. Griffith broke his foot in a pickup game, creating yet another major problem as the 1985-86 season got underway. But the club steadied itself with the play of rookie Malone, who averaged 14.9 points and 8.9 rebounds, and a rejuvenated Dantley, who scored at a 29.8 clip, second in the NBA to Atlanta's Dominique Wilkins (30.3). The effort resulted in a 42-40 showing, just the second winning record in the club's history, and a first-round playoff loss to the Dallas Mavericks.

Malone's big upside, however, had convinced Layden that he could trade the sometimes difficult Dantley, who had a style that left him holding the ball for seemingly interminable stretches in the halfcourt offense as he craftily set up his moves to the basket. It was great for individual, one-on-one battles, but it didn't do much for ball movement.

Unfortunately, the deal wasn't a great one. Detroit gave up Kelly Tripucka and Kent Benson in return for Dantley and a couple of second-round draft choices.

Freed from Dantley's domination of the ball, Malone averaged 21.7 ppg for 1986-87, and Stockton took a share greater of the point guard duties from Rickey Green. With a 44-38 record, the Jazz claimed a fourth consecutive playoff appearance. They even won the first two games in their opening series with Golden State, only to stumble and lose three in a row.

A pronounced lack of depth and experience was the problem, and those factors would evidence themselves in a pattern of late-season failures over the ensuing seasons. For 1987-88, the club struggled early, then found a rythmn that produced a franchise-best 47-35 record.

Malone's scoring (27.7 ppg) and rebounding (12.0 rpg) jumped to among the top five in the league, and he was voted to start in the 1988 NBA All-Star Game. Stockton, meanwhile, moved in as the team's starting point guard and responded to the promotion by breaking Isiah Thomas' NBA single-season record for assists with 1,128 (13.8 apg).

That spring, the Jazz dropped Portland in the first round of the playoffs, then got their first post-season test against the great Showtime Lakers, who were on their way to their fifth title of the decade. Utah forced the series to seven games before losing by 11 in the Forum.

Despite the loss, hopes ran high in Utah. The following fall, Layden abruptly decided the time had come to turn the team over to Sloan, his intense assistant. Sloan and his team answered with the franchise's first 50-win season and its second Midwest Division title, with a 51-31 record.

Malone and Mark Eaton (53) gave the Jazz an impressive defensive front in the late 1980s and early '90s.

The major difference seemed to be Sloan's demands for more defense, which was met with a 99.7 points-per-game effort by the players. In one game alone, Eaton blocked 14 shots. Malone, meanwhile, further established his stardom by netting MVP honors at the '89 All-Star Game with 28 points and nine rebounds for the West. Stockton averaged 13.6 assists and 3.21 steals. And Eaton was again named defensive player of the year.

Yet it all proved to be only so much window dressing when Sloan's first Jazz team fell in the first round to an undersized Warriors team led by Chris Mullin and Mitch Richmond.

A similar heartache awaited them in the 1990 playoffs after they had again boosted their regular-season record, this time to 55-27. The season was notable in that Stockton (who broke his own NBA record with 1,134 assists for an average of 14.5 per game) missed two games with a severely sprained ankle and Malone (who averaged 31 points per game) scored 61 points against Milwaukee. This time, though, the playoff agony came in the first round against Phoenix. The Jazz won the first two games, then lost the next three, including a two-point defeat in Game 5.

From there the litany of regular-season succcess and playoff failure continued season after season:

• In 1991, they finished 54-28 but lost to the Portland Trail Blazers, four games to one, in the Western Conference Semifinals. Stockton upped his NBA assists record with 1,164 (14.2 apg), surpassing the 1,000-assist mark for the fourth consecutive year while Malone averaged 29 points and 11.8 rebounds.

• For 1991-92, the Jazz said goodbye to the old Salt Palace and moved down the street to the brand new Delta Center, where they recorded a franchise-best 37-4 home record on their way to a 55-27 season. This time in the playoffs, they knocked off the LA Clippers and Seattle in the first two rounds, only to lose in six games to Clyde Drexler and the Portland Trail Blazers in the Western Conference Finals. Stockton led the league in assists (13.7 apg) and steals with 2.98 per game while Malone again finished second to Michael Jordan in the NBA scoring race with a 28.0 points-per-game average.

Their playoff agony was perhaps diminished a bit by the fact that both Stockton and Malone earned Olympic Gold medals as part of the U.S. Dream Team at the 1992 Summer Games in Barcelona, Spain. But the offseason success came with a cost. For 1992-93 Utah fell to a 47-35 record, then lost to the Seattle SuperSonics in the first round of the playoffs. The season had been highlighted by the Jazz hosting the All-Star Game in the Delta Center, where Stockton and Malone were named co-MVPs after leading the West to a 135-132 overtime victory. But both would have traded all that for a good playoff run.

The 1993-94 season brought 53 wins and a red-letter trade that sent Jeff Malone to the Philadelphia 76ers for dependable, deep-shooting Jeff Hornacek, which factored into the team's second decent playoff run. Utah returned to the conference finals by sweeping the San Antonio Spurs in the first round, then outlasting the Denver Nuggets in the second. The Jazz had gone up on Denver 3-0, then lost three games and had to hold on for a seventh game victory. However, Hakeem Olajuwan and the Houston Rockets were simply too strong in the post, and danced past Utah 4-1 on their way to the league championship.

The 1994-95 regular season was another special time in that the club claimed its first 60-win record and Stockton became the NBA's all-time assists leader. But the frustrations again won out, beginning in January when starting center Felton Spencer, who had replaed the retired Eaton, tore an Achilles tendon.

Strangely, Jerry Sloan's players noticed a newfound peace coming over their coach as the regular season wound to a close. "Jerry is doing the things now that I had always hoped he would do," Karl Malone said. "He'll still get in your face, but he'll also sit down on the bench and watch the game. It seems to me that he's enjoying the game more than he ever has.

"This is the best I've ever seen him coach, with a loss and a win. And now I can touch him on the shoulder during a game and he'll kind of smile at me sometimes, whereas in the past, he'd look at me like, 'What are you thinking about?' It's sort of neat to see him like that. He's still intense now, without a doubt. We got a motto: Once you suit up, you're ready to play. So he's intense, but now he also knows when to slack up a little bit, too."

As the playoffs began, this calm spread across the roster and combined with a series of winning streaks to give the Jazz perhaps the strongest confidence they'd ever had. "Do you think you can win it all?" a reporter asked John Stockton.

"Absolutely," he said. "We're just a good group of guys, hard-working guys, who are committed to each other and to winning."

The same reporter asked Stockton when he was going to slow down.

"Hopefully, never," the point guard replied. "Everything doesn't feel the way it felt 10 years ago. But I feel good. I feel I've been fortunate to stay somewhat injury-free. I'll keep my fingers crossed and keep playing."

"People say if you can't win it this year that you and Karl Malone might be getting too old," the reporter asked. "What do you think?"

"They also said that four years ago," Stockton said. "I think our best chances have been in the last two or three years, including this one. This is our best chance yet. We're just gonna try to take advantage of that and not worry about the other part."

Ultimately, it wasn't age, but luck, that cost the Jazz in the playoffs. They drew the defending champion Houston Rockets in the first round. The Rockets had struggled after a February trade that had sent power forward Otis Thorpe to Portland for Clyde Drexler. First, Drexler needed some time to adjust to his new teammates. Then, just as that adjustment was coming into line, Hakeem Olajuwon was sidelined for two weeks with anemia. Later, after Drexler began taking most of his playing time, Houston's Vernon Maxwell grew dissatisfied and left the team before the playoffs began.

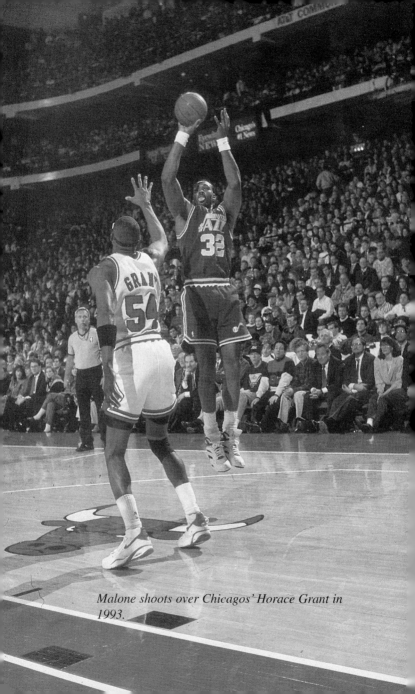

Malone shoots over Chicagos' Horace Grant in 1993.

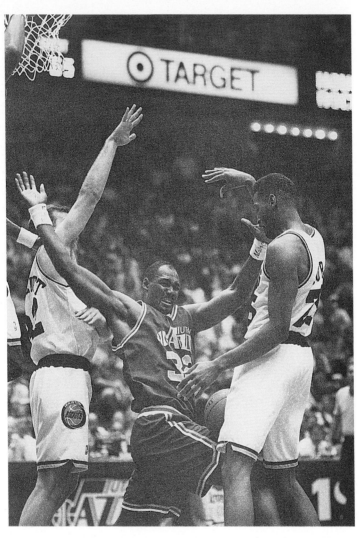

Houston Rockets' Pete Chilcutt, left, and Robert Horry, right, surround Karl Malone after he pulled down a rebound. Malone led the Jazz with 32 points in the best-of-five series in 1995.

AP Photo/David J. Phillip

Somehow, despite all the late-season turmoil, the Rockets came together during the playoffs. The Jazz had taken a 2-1 lead in the five-game series, but Houston managed to tie it with a key home win. Utah even had a solid lead late in the fourth quarter of Game 5 in Salt Lake City, but the Rockets closed in a swirl and won the series on a critical late shot.

A few weeks later, Jerry Sloan was at the league's rookie/free agent camp at Moody Bible Institute in Chicago, where he was offered condolences on yet another playoff loss. "It's all right," he said, not sounding entirely convincing. "It's just a f---ing ball game."

The '96 campaign produced another grand playoff run, but the familiar frustrating results in that the Jazz went all the way to the conference finals against Seattle only to lose in the seventh game on missed free throws.

"I've always thought our teams have had pride, our players have had pride," Sloan said in 1997. "We've experienced a lot of failures over the years. But it takes a lot of pride. You have to have a lot of pride in yourself to keep coming back and trying. I don't think our guys should be criticized for coming back and trying. Just because you haven't been successful, I don't think that makes you a bad person.

"You're talking about 10 years, you're talking about the kind of effort they've put in to get here. To me, that's important. Are you gonna teach your kid that if you don't win a championship you're gonna be a failure the rest of your life? I think there are lessons to be learned from everything you do, good or bad.

"The big factor in 1996," he said, "was that we missed a lot of free throws. If we had made our free throws in that final game against Seattle, we probably would have gone to the Finals. But we missed 'em. I don't worry about that. They didn't shoot 'em to miss. We just go on about our business."

Is there anything else he could do to get his team over the hump? he was asked.

"I hired a free throw coach," he said with a laugh.

As a young coach in Chicago, Sloan demanded competitive intensity.

THE COACH

When Jerry Sloan was an NBA player, he was known for his intensity, for being the kind of guy who would lay his heart on the line each and every game night. Karl Malone says that today, as coach of the Jazz, Sloan is still so intense most nights you can't touch him in the huddle.

"He's just a very competitive guy," Jazz broadcaster Hot Rod Hundley says of Sloan. "That's the way he played. That's the way he coaches. Jerry believes that you play as hard as you can," Hundley says. "If the players respond and play hard, that's all he cares about. If you've done everything you can, and you play it straight and compete, there's nothing more you can ask for. That's what he demands. That's why he's had great teams every year. He'll win at least 55 games every year. The players love him. He gets the ultimate out of 99 percent of these guys. He gets them to play hard."

John Stockton says that he owes a special debt to Sloan, his coach since 1988, the longest coaching tenure in the NBA today. It's not unusual for a coach and a point guard to burn out their relationship over the course of a single season. But not Sloan and Stockton. "He is a great guy, a great competitor," Stockton says. "He's been in the player's shoes. I've thoroughly enjoyed playing with him, playing for him. I hope that that situation never changes over my career. He has constant influence on me with the little things that he says, things that you need to relax about, things that you need to fire up for, things that he remembered as a player that maybe hit home with me."

Unfortunately, Sloan's experience as a player all too closely mirrors what his Jazz players have faced in recent seasons. Like the Chicago teams Sloan used to play for, his Utah squads often lacked a dominating center, which means they have played well each year during the regular season only to struggle in the playoffs.

Since 1989, Sloan's teams, featuring Stockton and Malone, have averaged 54 wins a season, and twice made it to the Western Conference Finals. But three other times they have lost in the first round of the playoffs. Such frustrations would probably get the best of lesser men. But Sloan doesn't even acknowledge the frustration, probably because acknowledging the frustration would mean acknowledging defeat. And he just won't do that.

MR. CHICAGO BULL

Hard as it may be to believe, long before Michael Jordan arrived on the scene, Jerry Sloan was known as Mr. Chicago Bull. At 6-6, he was a big guard, known for his defense and rebounding. Born into a family of 10 children and raised on a farm in the hardscrabble oil fields of southern Illinois, he played briefly at the University of Illinois and at Southern Illinois before transferring to Evansville in the early 1960s. There he led the team to two NCAA Division II national championships. Selected by the old Baltimore Bullets in the second round of the 1965 NBA draft, he played one season with Baltimore before being nabbed by Chicago in the 1966 expansion draft. Just a few games into that season, the Bullets approached Chicago about trading Sloan back to Baltimore. "No, a thousand times no," Bulls owner Dick Klein told them. "We're going to keep Jerry. I knock on wood every time I see him."

Over an 11-year NBA career, Sloan averaged 14 points and 7.4 rebounds, but his real contribution, his intense defense, escaped statistical analysis.

"Jerry was always an excitable person," said Johnny "Red"

Sloan challenged opponents with a rough and tumble style.

Kerr, who played with Sloan in Baltimore and coached him in Chicago. "I roomed with him in Baltimore on occasion. We'd play a game, and I'd go out for a couple of drinks and a sandwich. I'd come back at maybe one, two o'clock in the morning. I'd have the light off and be taking off my jacket. I'd see this glow of a cigarette in the dark. Jerry would be sitting up on the other bed, and he'd say, 'Red, remember that play in the third quarter?' I'd be getting ready for bed. I'd already had a couple of beers, and I'd forgotten about what happened in the third quarter because there was another game tomorrow. But he was so intense he wanted to know why we did certain things in certain situations. That really impressed me, and when I learned I was coming to Chicago as the coach, I knew he was gonna be one of the players I'd take in the expansion draft. He didn't get a lot of playing time with the Bullets, but I saw him every day in practice. Nobody wanted any part of him. I knew the intensity he had."

"When I was coming to Chicago," Sloan recalled, "Johnny Kerr told me, 'You're kind of like a spring that's wound too tight. You might just fly all over the place. You don't want to get that wound up.' I worked hard on trying not to get that way. But I had those tendencies. That's the only way I could compete. I wasn't good enough, in my mind, unless I maintained a high level of intensity.

"When I left Baltimore, I didn't know if I'd be able to play in this league or not. I was drafted fairly high, but I didn't play much in Baltimore and started to have doubts. Two weeks before I went to Chicago, my brother shot himself. I had gotten myself mentally ready to play. But I was concerned because I hadn't worked out for a week because of my brother's funeral. Fortunately, I was in great shape. I could play hard every minute in training camp, and I got a little confidence. From that point, Johnny Kerr gave me more confidence by allowing me to play."

The arrival of Dick Motta as Bulls coach in Sloan's third season in Chicago created a perfect match of competitive attitudes. Although he had never even seen an NBA game when he began coaching in the league, Motta was an absolute firebrand, the kind of guy who would punt a ball into the upper deck when he was angry over a referees call. One night he even spit on a ball and shoved it back into an official's hands.

"When we had our first training camp, it took about 10 minutes to recognize that he was very special," Motta said of Sloan. "There weren't many players that had his intensity. I began to depend on him more out of necessity than anything. It was a natural evolution. He approached his play like he was desperate. One time at a clinic I heard Jerry say, 'When I put the shoes on I get nervous because it might be the last time I'll ever get to put 'em on. So I want to play the best game I've ever played or have the best practice I've had.' He typified that his whole career."

If there was any part of his play that exemplified this intensity, it was his insistence on taking charges. Motta put together perhaps the most intimidating backcourt in the league in the 1970s when he teamed Sloan with Norm Van Lier, another hard-nosed defensive guard. Before long, opponents were complaining that Sloan and Van Lier were getting preferential treatment from the refs, that they would actually pull people on top of them to get charging fouls.

"There were no two tougher guards in basketball than Sloan and Van Lier," said Jeff Mullins, who played for the Golden State Warriors. "They were extremely competitive, very physical guys, the kind who would knock you down, then pick you up. They were always trying to draw the charge. I'll never forget. We had a rookie from North Carolina named Bobby Lewis. When we played the Bulls, I told him, 'Bobby, you gotta watch Sloan and Van Lier because when you give the ball up and cut through, they'll sorta get you by the jersey and pull you down with them.' Lewis sort of half-listened to me and went in the game. Sure enough, he comes down the first time, and Jerry pulled him right over. Charge. The next time Lewis came down the other side and cut through. Norm Van Lier stepped in front. Another charge. A

Sloan was a major factor on Chicago's team that made it to the Western Conference finals in 1975.

few minutes later Sloan got him again. Lewis got three straight charges without the ball and went bananas and had to sit down."

"Norm and I were very similar," Sloan admitted. "We were both crazy when it came to playing. Your hands have gotta be faster than the eye. We always had to have some means of taking peoples' minds off the game when they were on offense. Otherwise, they'd have just run by us like a layup drill if we'd let them play."

"A lot of those charges were legit," Van Lier says now. "A lot of people didn't have the guts to do it. A lot of those charges were hard, sure-enough, red-dog hits. But I took charges. I didn't pull you down. I wasn't strong enough to do that."

"I had the misfortune of having to play against Norm and Jerry Sloan," says Hall of Famer Nate "Tiny" Archibald, a guard for the old Cincinnati Royals. "Chicago was the toughest team to prepare for. We had some duels. They always outdid us. I remember we called our division the Black-and-Blue Division, mainly because we played against Chicago. I really didn't want them to physically beat me up, so I had to outrun those guys. A lot of people said they flopped on defense, but they were just guys that were glued to people.... I'd get past Norm. The next thing I knew, Jerry Sloan was in my face. They had that great mentality about guarding people. They had pride."

"Jerry was gonna give you a day's work every day he came into the gym," said Bulls teammate Bob Love. "As hard as he was, when he was on the floor, if you blew on him he would fall back and grab you on the way down to take the charge. The game I remember about Sloan, we were playing New York in Chicago Stadium. The Knicks had Willis Reed and Earl Monroe and Walt Frazier and those guys. Willis Reed got a rebound and threw it out and was gonna beat Tom Boerwinkle down the floor. He was hauling it down the floor. He had his head down, and when he looked up, Jerry Sloan was right there, man. He ran over Sloan. Charge! Willis fell on the floor and hurt his knee. He already had a bad knee. He looked at Jerry and said, 'Motherf----r, don't get in front of me again. You made me hurt my knee.' You know how guys talk. Sloan said, 'I ain't afraid of you.'

"Later in the game, Willis Reed got another rebound. He hauled off down the sideline again. This time he saw Jerry. Willis didn't go right, and he didn't go left. He ran over Jerry. When he hit Jerry, he walked all the way up to his head and scraped him and left Converse marks, from his forehead all the way down to his ear, man. All you saw was a red mark. And there was Willis saying, 'I told you not to get in front of me!' Sloan said, 'Mother------, I still ain't scared of you.'

"And the rest of the game, every time Willis got a rebound, he looked. He looked for Jerry. Jerry would have guys zigzagging down the floor, because you couldn't touch him. He was the greatest charge-taker that I have ever seen in my life. You couldn't touch him, because he'd just fall back. Unbelievable.

"Jerry would make guys so mad," Love said. "Right now he would be considered the all-time greatest defensive player the game has ever known if he was playing on TV. He would have every kid in America copying that style. I loved the way the guy played. I was so happy I played with him and Norm Van Lier, because they made other guys so angry the way they played. The two best defensive guards in the history of the game, and they played on the same team. The best. Norm and Jerry were out there like two rats, and if the ball fell on the floor, it was like a piece of cheese. Those guys would undercut you, overcut you, clip you, do anything they could to get that ball. And they would get it, boy. And Dick Motta just loved it. He loved those guys. They really kept us pumped up."

"Jerry and I used to have our battles when we played against each other," said former player/coach Matt Guokas, who played with and against Sloan. "Jerry is a unique defender in that he did not get up and put a lot of pressure on you, but he played angles, played position very well. He would make you do a lot of things

Sloan getting his number 4 retired by the Bulls.

you didn't want to do, but he didn't do it with pressure. Jerry was an excellent team defensive player and rebounder. When I played against him, we would get tangled up underneath the basket. There would be some elbow throwing, and we got in each other's face a couple of times. I was very happy to be on the same team with him. He was very demanding that you did certain things defensively, that you played hard, and that you got on the floor for loose balls and stepped up and took charges.

"That, of course, was the other thing about playing against Jerry," Guokas said. "He used to flop. He'd pull you on top of him and get you in foul trouble with a lot of charges. You wouldn't get away with that in today's game. There's still a lot of flopping that goes on, but you couldn't put your arms around a guy and pull him down. Let me put it this way: They got away with it when I was on the other team, but when I was on the Bulls it seems they got called for it. Jerry was the consummate team player. Everyone that played with Jerry respected him. He was always in pain with a very bad groin injury. He would not get it stretched out before practice, yet he would go out and practice very hard for about an hour, which was all you could get out of anybody."

"Jerry and Norm Van Lier would just jump in front of you," said former Bulls guard Bob Weiss. "Jerry would take the hit. His weight would be on his heels, so it didn't take a whole lot to knock him over. But a charge is a charge. I think the term 'flopping' was basically an excuse for these guys they were drawing the fouls from. Jerry and Van Lier were very, very good at it. Jerry mostly. He was always getting in somebody's way and taking the punishment."

Like the Jazz teams Sloan later coached, the Bulls of the 1970s—featuring Love and Chet Walker at forward, Tom Boerwinkle and Clifford Ray at center, and Sloan and Van Lier in the backcourt—would regularly win 50 games a season.

"Nobody could quite figure out why we were so successful," recalled former Bulls general manager Pat Williams, now an executive with the Orlando Magic. "Dick Motta used to say, 'When people look at this team, they forget the one key ingredient—the size of Jerry Sloan's heart.' Jerry Sloan was just fearless. His body would take such a pounding. In all my 28 years in the league, the player I most admire is Sloan. I've never been around a greater competitor, a more focused guy, a guy who cared as much . . .

"He's the only guy I've ever seen who played with his fists," Williams said. "He had huge hands. When he'd go for the ball on a steal, he'd punch it. He'd punch the ball right out of your hands. There's never been another Sloan. Never will be."

"My second year in Chicago, we had to make up a game," Dick Motta recalled. "We had a game snowed out, and the league put it right at the end of the season. We had to play five games in five nights, and we needed to win four of them to make the playoffs. We beat Boston and Detroit in Chicago, then beat Milwaukee in a game played at Madison, Wisconsin. But with about a minute to go in the game, Lew Alcindor came out from behind a screen and knocked Jerry down. Jerry broke two ribs and separated his sternum. We had to bus down from Madison to O'Hare Airport after that Sunday afternoon game to catch a flight to Omaha to play Cincinnati for a game Monday night. So we had a doctor meet us at the airport. He basically told us that Sloan shouldn't go, that he should stay home. But Jerry insisted on going just to be with the team. We just needed one more win. The next day I went to the arena, and Sloan was there. He said, 'I couldn't sleep. I've been walking around. I've found this little corset thing. Let me warm up.'

"I said, 'No, I'm not gonna let you,'" Motta recalled. "He said, 'Coach, you gotta let me warm up.' So he warmed up and I went back to the locker room. Later, I came out a little early, and he came up to me and said, 'You know I've never asked you to do one thing. I've never told you to do one thing. I'm gonna ask one favor now.'

"I said, 'What's that, Jerry?'

"He said, 'If I were you, I'd start me.'

"I started him," Motta said, "and he couldn't raise his arm. Chet Walker and I had to stretch the uniform to get him in it. His ribs were broken, but he just wouldn't quit. We were down three early in the second half, and Cincinnati called a quick timeout. In the huddle, Jerry said, 'C'mon guys, let's go. We've come from 33 down before.'

"I looked up at the clock and said, 'Jerry, what's wrong?'

"He said, 'Oh, I thought we were down 33.'

"The pain was so excruciating he was incoherent," Motta said. "He was going on an empty tank. We won the game in overtime, and made the playoffs. I was able to rest Jerry the last game, and he played in the playoffs. So it was easy to build a team around that type of performance. He had a bad game once. I think his sister-in-law had died, and he went down to Evansville to the funeral and wasn't going to make it back. But he rented a small plane and got there about three minutes before tipoff. Chet Walker looked at him and said, 'I thought you weren't gonna play tonight.'

"He said, 'I couldn't miss it.'

"Chet said, 'You're a hell of a guy, Jerry.'

"And that's how everyone perceived Jerry," Motta said. "No coach and player had a relationship like Jerry and I had. It was very special. He was my sounding board, my assistant coach the first four years when I didn't have an assistant coach. So I would bounce trades off of him. I bounced all of our deals off of Jerry. I felt it was more his team than it was mine. He was an incredible guy. He still is."

"Sloan and Dick were like brothers," former Bull Gar Heard said. "It was like blood. They had such a great love for each other. Even now. I don't think anything could come between them. Sloan was the one guy who would play every night. On some nights I didn't see how he walked out on the floor. He was so banged up with his knees and stuff. But every night he came on the floor you knew he was gonna get it on."

"They retired Sloan's number 4 in Chicago," Motta said. "I

Sloan during his days coaching the Bulls.

don't know if he'll ever be in the Hall of Fame, but he should be."

Sloan and his Bulls teammates battled their entire career trying to reach the NBA Finals. The closest they came to playing for the championship was the 1975 Western Conference Finals, where they took a 3-2 advantage over the Golden State Warriors.

"That was a great series against Golden State," Sloan recalled. "We played about seven guys, but most of the starters played about 40 to 45 minutes a night in the playoffs. That was the frustrating thing. People said we were too old. We were in our 30s. But I don't know if anybody 21 could have played as hard as we did for the minutes we played. Looking back on it, I think the excitement and the moment was something nobody had dealt with before. I think we probably got ourselves so high that we just couldn't get it done."

Ironically, the Bulls had traded Clifford Ray to the Warriors for center Nate Thurmond, the dominating center they thought they needed. But Ray's rebounding and defense played a key role in defeating his former teammates. The Bulls had a solid lead in Game 7, but lost down the stretch and sat exhausted in the locker room afterward.

"That was a pretty sad day for me," Sloan said.

His playing career ended a few months later with a knee injury early in the 1975-76 season. He was a two-time All-Star and four times was named to the league's All-Defensive first team and twice to the All-Defensive second team. After his playing days, he accepted the job as head coach at Evansville, his alma mater, the team that as a three-time All-American Sloan had led to a 29-0 season and two national titles. But he changed his mind and resigned five days later. That fall of 1977, just months after his resignation, the Evansville team and coaching staff were killed in a plane crash. Just a week earlier he had visited with the Evansville players when they played in Chicago against DePaul, and the incident left him badly shaken for many months.

"It comes across my mind every morning I go to work," says

Sloan. "Evansville had that tragic accident ..."

Instead of coaching in college, Sloan became an assistant with the Bulls and was named the team's head coach in 1979. The owners had picked him, thinking he was the man to lead the team

Sloan talks to a writer during the 1997 playoffs.

out of its years of frustration. But he had trouble adjusting his intensity.

"There was a real sense of excitement with his hiring," recalled Tim Hallam, the Bulls' longtime PR man. "The owners thought Jerry Sloan would be the one guy who could rectify this stuff. But they just kept bringing in young guys and draft picks, and none of them worked out."

"I wasn't ready to be a coach, obviously," Sloan says. "But since I'd played here I figured if I had the right people around me to help me out, I had a better feeling for all the things that were going on here and some of the problems you were gonna have to deal with."

"Jerry was a wild man," recalled former Bulls trainer Mark Pfeil. "His idea was, things don't have to be complicated if you lay your heart on the line every night. And that's the way he coached."

"Some guys did not like Jerry," said former Bull Ronnie Lester, now a scout for the Lakers. "Not that he was a tough guy to play for. But he demanded things of his players. He would get in players' faces and challenge them personally, and a lot of players did not like that and did not take well to it."

"You have to have intensity to a certain point," Sloan says of coaching, "but it can be very damaging to you. The intensity I had as a player, it was hard to put aside as a coach. Early in my career, any question from other people seemed to be more of a challenge than anything else. I probably took it that way. That was very difficult for me. I wanted everything to be perfect. I didn't realize that it wasn't going to be."

Sloan's first Chicago team finished 30-52, and for his second year, the team brought in free agent forward Larry Kenon, who had averaged about 20 points and 10 rebounds for San Antonio. Almost immediately, the two began feuding.

"Jerry was such a straight-forward, stand-up guy," Hallam said. "This was in the days before coaches began using the phoniness and coddling and bull that it took to keep players happy. Jerry wasn't coddled as a person, didn't expect it, and wasn't going to give it. I think he got along with his kind of players. He didn't get along with Larry Kenon. When I met Larry Kenon, I said, 'Hello, Larry.' He said, 'Larry is my slave name. People call me K. or Dr. K.'

"Sloan threw a chair and had to get his attention," Hallam said. "I think Kenon pissed Jerry off quite a bit and was really frustrating for Jerry. But Kenon wasn't about to change."

Sloan benched Kenon, then proceeded to coach the Bulls into the 1981 playoffs, where they upset the New York Knicks in the first round and lost to the Boston Celtics in the conference semi-finals. But the next season, when the team started 19-32, general manager Rod Thorn fired Mr. Chicago Bull.

"Firing Jerry was one of the toughest things I've ever done because I have a lot of respect for him," Thorn says now. "He works very hard, is a stand-up guy. He doesn't make excuses. He does everything he can do and is always there. He never bails out."

Hallam remembers that the day Sloan was fired, he agreed to meet with reporters. Sloan answered every single question that day, and made no excuses for his lack of success.

"They'd always paid me on the first and the 15th," Sloan said of the Bulls. "That's one of the things I'd always appreciated. That's life. Because we're in sports we think we deserve a little bit more than that, but really we don't."

The toughest part of the firing was explaining to his kids that everything was going to be all right, that the world wasn't going to end just because he wasn't with the Bulls.

Sure enough, he landed a job coaching in the Continental Basketball Association. Then Frank Layden brought him to Utah as an assistant coach, where he has remained ever since.

"I was very lucky to work for Frank Layden," Sloan says. "I've gotten a lot funnier. Actually, it was very difficult when I went to work in Frank's position. But I learned more basketball and more about people from Frank Layden than I have any time in my life."

Each season in Utah as spring comes to the Rockies, Sloan has faced the same circumstances, a successful regular season capped by an immense playoff challenge. Deep in Sloan's gut each year, there's probably a terrible knot of anxiety. As Johnny Kerr recalled him as a young player, Sloan probably still sits alone at night after a loss, smoking in the dark, thinking about errant plays. Wayne Boultinghouse, his friend and college teammate, says Sloan is driven by a desire to "never be perceived as failing." But he'll never admit to any such anxiety.

"I'm not obsessed with basketball," Sloan says. "I love it, and it's been great to me. But I'm not totally consumed by it."

"He definitely doesn't get his due," says Houston Rockets coach Rudy Tomjanovich. "Jerry's been a great leader for that team, and he does it the right way: He doesn't make himself the focal point."

Indeed, he stands apart in a world of coaching dandies like Pat Riley and Rick Pitino. "I don't really have anything to do with it," he says of his team's success. "It's up to our players. I tell them, 'I can tell you how to run the floor, but I can't do it for you.' Our guys know pretty much what we expect. Not that we always get it, but as long as they play hard and try to do what we ask 'em, it's pretty simple. That's why my guys have kept my job for me."

The contradiction in all of this is that no NBA coach is more insistent on maintaining competitiveness as a standard. For example, his all-important statistic has little to do with points or rebounds. Instead, it's "deflections," the number of times his players make contact with the ball on defense, which to Soan indicates how close his players are to their men. "It's not an official stat," he says. "It's just something goofy we do. I use it to measure to see if we're close to anybody. I've always felt like it's important. If a guy's up close to who he's guarding, he might get his hand on the basketball. The guy on the other team might

For Stockton, Soan was the perfect coach.

throw one away 'cause he knows you're close. At least, you're close enough to the guy to foul him if you're getting the hand on the basketball once in a while. And that's been a pretty big determining factor with us.

"At least, I know if a guy gets up around his man and he's committed a few fouls, he's at least close to the guy. That helps a little bit. At least, your body's alive, and when your body comes alive you're able to shoot the basketball better."

Deflections are a function of hustle, which is a function of motivation, yet Sloan disdains the idea that a coach fills the role of motivator, mostly because the concept eats away at the individual athlete's commitment and responsibility to compete. "Motivation, I think that's the most overused word in sports," he says. "I don't know how you motivate anybody. You have to motivate yourself. That's the only way I look at it. People say, 'Well, I talked to this guy and I really got him fired up.' The guy fired himself up. And everybody wants the credit for it."

It's the same insistence on responsibility that fires him up as a coach. "No one is going to put any more pressure on me than what I put on myself," Sloan says. "There's nobody, no newspaper guy, no TV guy, nobody's gonna put more pressure on me than me. They can say what they want and do what they want. I put a lot of pressure on myself. And I don't always do the right thing either.

"I put some of the wrong guys in there at times. I should be criticized as much for that as the other part of it. And I don't have a problem with that. I've made a lot of mistakes."

Overcomplicating the game is not one of them, however. From his short practices to his lenient policies on family issues, he takes real efforts to make sure the process doesn't smother his players and douse their fire. "I don't screw around in practice, I'll tell you that," he says. "I never played for a coach who practiced over an hour and 15 minutes. I couldn't sit there that long. I figured if I worked hard for an hour and 15 minutes, that's enough, if you put

Stockton has made the championship his quest.

enough energy into it. That includes stretching and running and loosening up. I've never had long practices. Maybe in training camp, we had to talk and listen to all the bullshit to start with. That takes a little longer. For the most part, I've never had long practices.

"This is a long, drawn-out process to me. I want these guys to have long careers. That wouldn't be fair to John Stockton, Karl Malone and those guys. Their career is more important than mine. I think it's important that you respect that with your players. That's why I've tried to keep them a long time.

"There's 29 different coaches in this league," Sloan says, "and they've all got something different. They're all probably right. I'm probably wrong more than anybody. But you have to be yourself. I put a lot of trust in the people I work with. They have a lot of responsibility from a coaching standpoint. I think everybody knows that. I do less coaching, as far as coaching itself, than I did when I was an assistant to Frank Layden. Frank taught me a lot about this game. Don't overcoach. That's the first thing he told me."

Yet, strangely, Sloan does admit that in an age where coaches have turned the full reins over to their players on the floor, he still insists on calling plays from the sidelines, even with a point guard like Stockton at the wheel. "I've always done that," Sloan says. "I've always called plays. I don't know if that's right or not. Everybody's entitled to their own opinion. I've always felt like with John, he likes to know where everybody is on the floor. Sometimes if you don't call plays, you play a little bit helter-skelter; I think that takes away from his effectiveness.

"Plus I've always subscribed to the idea that if a guy's a 50-percent shooter, I like for him to have the ball more than a 30-percent shooter. Sometimes if you call a certain play, you know the ball is gonna go to that position. Now, you have to react to that if the opponent double teams or something. The guys have always accepted the fact that I call plays."

To Jerry Sloan, the answer to the challenge is as simple as it was decades ago, when he was a kid on that southern Illinois farm, after his father had died, leaving a family of 10 to fend for themselves.

You lay your heart on the line.

Night after night. Game after game. Then you get up the next day and start it all over again.

Rodman and Malone get tangled.

The Rise of The Utah Jazz

SHOW ME THE TITLE!

"It's been fun to watch our players. It's exciting from a coaching standpoint because you're trying to win it. You have to zero in on everything that's going on. It's exciting to see what guys are going to come to play. I really think this is the most important time in their lives, from a player's standpoint."

-- Jerry Sloan

Once again, John Stockton and Karl Malone came into an NBA season and played every game, night after night shaking off the aches and sprains and bruises and illnesses that regularly sidelined many players in the league. Once again, the effort paid off, lifting them yet another notch higher on basketball's competitive scale, higher than they had ever gone before.

The 1996-97 regular season proved to be a paragon for the Jazz, and not just because Malone, after years of impressive performances, was finally recognized as the league's Most Valuable Player (during the season, he became one of only five players in league history to register better than 25,000 points and 10,000 rebounds). More importantly, it was a benchmark season because the club had at last developed the depth necessary to compete for the league championship.

Obviously, Stockton, who averaged 14.4 points and 10.5 assists per game, and Malone, who scored at a 27.4 clip with 9.9 rebounds, remained the heart of the Utah offense. But Jeff Hornacek averaged 14.5 points, and Bryon Russell contributed 10.8 points per game. The other starter, center Greg Ostertag, averaged better than seven points and seven rebounds, while reserves Antoine Carr, Shandon Anderson, Howard Eisley, Adam Keefe, Chris Morris and Greg Foster all played a substantial role in the club racking up a franchise-best 64 wins (including a 38-3 home record) to finish just five back of the streaking Chicago Bulls. The Jazz were the best-shooting team in the NBA, lacing in an astounding .504 of their attempts.

The aggregate of their efforts was a machinelike team countenance, with all of the role players fitting in as key parts, and with Malone as the huge power. "We're not a great defensive team," Sloan said, "but we do all right for the talent level and the guys we have. Karl Malone is the most overpowering guy we have, obviously, and he's very overpowering. But we need everybody to play and play within the same concept."

Malone opened the season with big performances and kept them coming month after month, an effort that ignited a special spark with Utah's fans, who, as the season progressed became a chorus in the Delta Center, chanting "MVP!" after Malone's outstanding plays. It was a refrain soon picked up by journalists and opponents around the NBA.

"Karl Malone never seems to run down," Lakers coach Del Harris said after Malone worked for 37 points in a November win in Los Angeles. "For us to have won tonight, we would have had to play our best game of the year."

By spring, there was a growing call for Malone to finally be named the league's MVP, although Chicago's Michael Jordan was in the process of leading his team to 69 wins after having carried them to a league-record 72 wins in 1995-96. "Michael has kept the Bulls there," Houston's Charles Barkley, himself a former MVP, said in April as Malone racked up an unprecedented 10th straight 2,000-point season. "But I think Karl deserves it."

Barkley's comments echoed a host of others:

"I don't know if there are any power forwards in the league who can put the game on the line like Karl Malone," Atlanta

Howard Eisley goes to the hole against Chicago as teammates Bryon Russell (3) and Greg Ostertag look on.

center Dikembe Mutombo had observed a week earlier.

In March, Indiana coach Larry Brown had watched Malone disassemble the Pacers and told reporters afterward, "He just dominated the game. He got the ball where he wanted, he got whatever shot he wanted, he did everything. That's why he's one of the greatest players in the league."

"Consistent as running water ..." Detroit coach Doug Collins told *Sports Illustrated* that same month.

"He is a quiet star has who has accepted who he is and where he is with a humility you must admire ..." agreed Seattle's coach George Karl.

His effort led the Jazz to their first-ever best record in the Western Conference, meaning they had the home court advantage throughout the conference playoffs for the first time in their history.

In the end, the effort and accomplishments meant that the 1996-97 season would come down to a contest between the bitter and the sweet. The sweet, of course, was that Stockton and Malone carried the Jazz to the brink of their dreams, creating a hope that had fans across the state of Utah screaming, "Show Me The Title!"

With every game of the regular season and every round of the playoffs it became perfectly clear that Stockton, Malone and company were going to do everything in their power to make it happen.

In the process, they victimized Los Angeles twice. In the first round, the Jazz dispatched the Clippers in three quick games. Then came the young and infinitely athletic Lakers, led by Shaquille O'Neal, Nick Van Exel and Eddie Jones. Utah claimed the first two games at home, then traveled to Los Angeles for a 20 point whipping by the brash young Lakers during which Malone made just two of 20 field goal attempts.

Despondent, Malone phoned his wife Kay, a former Miss

Shandon Anderson and Jeff Hornacek try to trap Michael Jordan in the 1997 championship series.

Idaho, afterward and told her how awful it had been.

"What's 2-for-20?" she asked.

The reply jolted a laugh out of Malone and made him realize that he needed a break to forget about the pressure. So he and three teammates headed to the nearby LA beaches for a bike ride. "In 12 years, I might have left my hotel room five or six times," Malone said. "But this time I just wanted to get out. So I spent my Friday at the beach. I told my wife, and she said, 'You never

Malone found trouble at the line in Chicago.

go for a bike ride.' But I guess there comes a time for everything.
We saw a guy with all these broken bottles on the ground, and he
was jumping off a chair right onto the bottles. I said, 'And I
thought I had a bad day.'"

Malone responded with 42 points in Game 4, which Utah won

by 15, and the Lakers were headed down in flames. The series
returned to Utah for a fifth game, which the Jazz won in overtime.
"Karl Malone was two for 20 one night in Los Angeles in the
playoffs," Sloan would say later, with a slight smile. "You know
what? The Lakers came out and guarded him close the next night.

If that isn't respect, I don't know what is. You always have to come back to what you believe in. All we ever have is luck. But I like my chances a lot better when Stockton and Malone are running things."

In the conference finals, the challenge was a powerful Houston team, led by Hakeem Olajuwon, Clyde Drexler, Barkley and Kevin Willis. In the past, the Rockets had always victimized the Jazz, and this year the addition of Barkley and Willis made them even deadlier.

On the eve of the series, it was announced that Malone had been named the league's MVP. In the moments before Game 1, he was presented the trophy in a quick ceremony. He took the award without saying so much as a word. "I didn't want to draw any more attention to the MVP than had already been on me," he explained later. "They wanted me to say something, and I said absolutely not. I wanted to do this quick so I could stay focused on the game."

That proved impossible. He scored 21 on only six of 16 shooting, but Utah claimed a team win, 101-86. The Rockets looked exhausted after having battled Seattle in the other semifinal.

Game 2 proved little better for Houston, as Barkley's frustrations flashed. At one point, he hammered Stockton with a flagrant foul and afterward said he was "trying to separate his shoulder or break his rib."

When the post-game interview session with reporters broke into chuckles at the comment, Barkley frowned and said, "I was serious."

Asked about Barkley, Stockton told reporters, "Whatever. That's my comment on what he did and what he said — whatever."

The Rockets won big in Houston when the series shifted there for Game 3, and Game 4 came down to the final seconds with the score tied. Sloan decided to double team the Rockets in the post, leaving Houston's Eddie Johnson wide open to hit the game-

Greg Foster provided depth.

winning three-pointer.

Tied, the series moved back to Utah for Game 5, where the Jazz took full advantage of the home court and their crowd noise for a five-point win.

Then the Rockets re-established their power in Game 6 back in the Summit. With 6:45 left in the game, Houston led 90-77, and it appeared the series was headed back to Utah for a big squeeze in Game 7. But Stockton pushed the competitiveness to the level that Sloan loves over the next six minutes. He scored Utah's final nine points (to finish with 25 and 13 assists).

With two minutes left, the Rockets led 98-91. Bryon Russell then hit a three-pointer, and from there Stockton took over with two layups to tie it at 98. Barkley pushed Houston back up with two free throws, but Stockton got into the lane and tied it with 22.4 seconds to go. Drexler missed a 12-footer on Houston's possession, leaving just enough time for one last Jazz execution. Bryon Russell inbounded the ball, Malone set a pick, and Stockton rifled in a trey that sent Utah to the league championship series for the first time in three decades of team history, 103-100. He thrust his arms to the rafters as Malone, Hornacek and the rest of the team mobbed him. The Summit crowd sat stunned and silent.

"I'm just so glad it went in," gushed the normally stoic point guard.

"We said we wanted to win it here," Malone told reporters. "It makes it that much sweeter because they've knocked us out of it a couple of times."

Watching the game on TV back in Chicago was 75-year-old Bulls assistant Tex Winter. "I like the way Utah plays," the Bulls' offensive coordinator said. "They're effective, and they have a system. They're a lot like us. They've been together a long time. They stay within the framework of their system."

Russell did a solid defensive job on Jordan in the Championship.

FINALLY

Experienced as they were, the Jazz veterans weren't quite prepared for the hype of the NBA Finals, which opened in Chicago on Sunday, June 1, 1997, with more than a thousand journalists from around the world credentialed to cover the event.

"It was different than anything any of us have ever experienced," Stockton woud explain later. "I've mentioned a couple of times, getting off the bus in Chicago that first day and being inundated by the media. Not that it affected the game, I thought we came out and played with a lot of confidence and were not affected by all that. But, it is an indicator of the adjustments you have to make going into something that big and that new."

"I never thought we'd ever get there," Sloan admitted.

Sloan himself provided another emotional reason for Chicago to greet Utah in the Finals. There, in the United Center before Game 1, was Sloan, hands jammed in pockets, awaiting the introductions, scanning the Chicago crowd, better heeled and not as rabid as the one that used to cheer him on in old Chicago Stadium. Sloan slapped fives as his starters stepped out for introductions. Then he shook hands with all the subs and all his assistants. The moment he had waited a career for was about to begin. He had virtually cut his heart out to get to the Finals for eight seasons as a player in Chicago. In this most delicious of ironies, he had finally reached it, to face his old team, the team that had retired his number 4, now hanging as a banner at the far west end of the building, one of only two jerseys honored in the United Center rafters, the other being Bob Love's number 10. Sloan and Love had been teammates on Bulls teams that put together a run of 50-win seasons in the 1970s and came achingly close to playing their way into the 1975 championship series.

"It's been fun to watch our players," Sloan would say later. "It's exciting from a coaching standpoint because you're trying to win it. You have to zero in on everything that's going on. It's exciting to see what guys are going to come to play. I really think this is the most important time in their lives, from a player's standpoint."

The view of Sloan's banner was largely obscured from his seat on the visitor's bench at the east end of the building, which for Sloan was just as well, because he wanted to put all those old ghosts, all those old Bulls frustrations, out of his mind.

It was, however, a night for legends. Muhammad Ali was introduced before tipoff, sporting a colorful leather Bulls jacket, prompting the building to erupt with chants of "Ali! Ali! Ali!"

Speaking of heavyweights, Malone had narrowly edged Jordan, the prime contender and four-time winner of the award, in the MVP voting. Jordan said he didn't mind the Jazz power forward getting the individual honor so long as the Bulls claimed the team championship at the end of playoffs. Now the stars and their respective teams were meeting to settle the matter on the court, with fans in both Chicago and Utah eager to seize on the issue, chanting MVP! when one or the other stepped to the free throw line at key moments throughout the series.

Jordan had his familiar compadres, Scottie Pippen, Dennis Rodman, Luc Longley, Toni Kukoc, Ron Harper and the other role players who had helped Chicago to the '96 title, their fourth in six years. Now only Sloan and his team stood between them and a fifth championship.

The Jazz rushed out to a solid start in Game 1 by throwing quick double teams at Jordan and working the boards hard, good enough for a quick Utah lead. Lest the Jazz get too confident, the Luv A Bulls issued a reminder by performing a "We Are The Champions Of The World" routine during a timeout.

From its earliest action, the series showed a gentlemanly tone, one not always seen in NBA championship play. When Antoine Carr fouled Chicago's Randy Brown early in the proceedings, the Utah forward walked over to check on Brown, patted him on the back and helped him up. Yet even the feel-good atmosphere couldn't alleviate the tension, evidenced by Chicago's 40 percent shooting in the first half. Utah was slightly better at 44 percent, with Stockton scoring 11 and Malone 10. Utah's Bryon Russell hit a three pointer just before the buzzer to give the Jazz a 42-38 halftime lead.

Jeff Hornacek scored 11 points in the third period to help keep Utah in the lead, except for a brief run by Chicago that netted a one-point edge. The fourth opened with Utah clutching a two-point lead in the face of a mountain of Chicago's trademark pressure.

Urging the Jazz on was a vocal pocket of Utah fans in the United Center's east end zone upper deck. Even Bulls' coach Phil Jackson couldn't understand the quiet anxiety of the home crowd. At one point, as the game narrowed to a close, he turned in his seat on the bench and urged the fans to turn loose a little energy to get the Bulls over the hump.

Mostly, though, the tension tightened the atmosphere down the stretch. With just under eight minutes to go, Stockton hit a jumper, pushing the Utah lead to 70-65, which Chicago's Ron Harper promptly answered with a trey. Surging on that momentum, the Bulls managed to stay close and even took a one-point edge on a Longley jumper with three minutes left.

Malone responded with two free throws, but Harper snuck inside for an offensive rebound moments later and passed out to Pippen for a trey that put Chicago up, 81-79. For most teams, that would have been enough pressure for a fold, but Stockton hit a three of his own with 55 seconds left to make it 82-81, Utah.

Then at the 35.8-second mark, Hornacek fouled Jordan, who stepped to the line with the building chanting MVP. He hit the first free throw to tie it, then missed the second, sending the crowd back to its nervous silence. The Jazz promptly spread the floor and worked the shotclock. As it ran down, Stockton missed a trey.

Who can forget what happened next? Certainly Malone never will. He hustled to track down a critical offensive rebound with

The Bulls' defense tried to force Stockton to the outside.

seconds to go and was fouled.

As Malone prepared to shoot his free throws, Scottie Pippen whispered in his ear, "The Mailman doesn't deliver on a Sunday." To ensure that, the crowd raised a ruckus. His first shot rolled off the rim, and the building exploded in celebration. He stepped back from the line in disgust, then stepped back up, wiped his hand on his shirt, dropped eight short dribbles and missed again, bringing yet another outburst of delight from the crowd as the Bulls controlled the rebound with 7.5 seconds left.

"I'm from Summerfield, Louisiana, and we don't have any excuses down there. So I'm not going to use any," Malone would say later. "It was agonizing, but I won't dwell on it. They were big free throws, but it shouldn't have come down to that... I just didn't make them."

The looks were long in the Jazz huddle during the ensuing timeout. Now they had to defend against Jordan on a buzzer beater. Amazingly, they decided not to double-team him.

Sloan thought of how he had chosen to double-team in Game 3 of the Houston series, only to see Eddie Johnson knock down the game-winner. So he told his players, "We're gonna try and play in front of everybody and make 'em shoot over the top. You got a 50-percent chance he'll miss it."

Pippen inbounded the ball to Kukoc, who quickly dumped it off to Jordan, who executed a move on Bryon Russell and broke free just inside the three-point line on the left side. The entire building froze there for an instant upon the release of the shot. When it swished, 21,000 fans leaped instantly in exhultation, a strange sight of simultaneous overstimulation, almost like something you'd see on the Nature Channel, when the cilia on the underbelly of some sea creature get zapped by the light.

The shot gave the Bulls the win, 84-82, and the Jazz sank instantly, knowing they had just lost any hopes they had of controlling the series.

Asked afterward by a cheeky reporter his opinion on who

deserved the MVP, Malone replied, "What do you want me to say, Michael Jordan, just like everybody else? Obviously, it's Michael Jordan, no matter what Karl Malone says or not. Michael wanted the ball at the end and made the shot, and it's hard to argue with that."

Jordan had finished with 31 points on 13 of 27 shooting while Malone rebounded after missing seven of his first eight shots to score 23 on the night with 15 rebounds.

"I think anyone watching anywhere in the world knew who would take the shot," Stockton said of the game-winner.

"We ran the play to perfection," observed Pippen, who finished with 27 despite his sore foot. "We gave Michael the ball and told him don't leave them any time on the clock. He just eyed it out and took the shot he felt good about."

"As I was watching the clock and the defense—I was surprised Russell was on me because he hadn't guarded me all game — I felt they may double-team," Jordan said. "But the double-team never came, and I knew I was in a one-on-one situation. I crossed over, he went for the steal, and I moved to my left and put up the jump shot."

"After it was all over, I felt like maybe I should have gone and doubled Michael Jordan. All right?" Sloan said later. "I didn't want to go do it in Houston. I didn't want to go double. So we go double anyway and leave a guy open, Eddie Johnson, and he makes a three-point shot. He made the shot. I felt better about that (in Chicago) than I did leaving the guy wide open in Houston, even though it was Michael Jordan. So they can criticize me or whatever. I don't have any problem with it. I did what I felt was right, and I slept good the night after it was all over."

Chicago's defense had forced Utah into a playoff-high 18 turnovers, including seven from Stockton. The Jazz point guard finished with 16 points and 12 assists. "The first game is always the toughest -- I don't care what anybody says," Jordan said. "Utah came in and played extremely well. I'm sure they're going to take a moral victory from tonight's game."

He was speaking tongue-in-cheek, of course. There are no moral victories in championship play.

The Bulls opened Game 2 three nights later as loose as the Jazz were tight, and the scoring showed it. Jordan hit a jumper, then Pippen finished off a Harper back-door pass with a reverse, and moments later Longley broke free for an enthusiastic stuff. Like that, the Jazz were in a maze and couldn't find their way out. Sloan was amazed at how quickly his team was overwhelmed.

Long known for their sadism, the Bulls game management people had set up Part II of Malone's little chamber of personal horrors by declaring it clacker night and passing out noisemakers by the thousands to fans as they entered the building. A similar ploy had completely unnerved Miami's Alonzo Mourning in the first round of the '96 playoffs. Now it was the Mailman's turn.

When Longley fouled Malone 90 seconds into the game, the clackers were waiting and rattled him into two free throw misses. Two minutes later, when Malone went to the line again with the Jazz trailing 8-1, the whole barn was rattling like a giant playpen. This time, Malone stepped up and hit both. Given a momentary rush of confidence, Utah closed to 14-13 at the 4:41 mark of the first period.

Jordan was afire, though, and quickly squashed any momentum with a trey and a jumper. Then he fed Steve Kerr for a pair of treys, and like that, Chicago had stretched the lead to 25-15 with 1:30 left in the period, which had 21,000 fans on their feet clapping and pounding to "Wooly Bully." The crowd's timidity in Game 1 had prompted NBC analyst Bill Walton to quip that the only noise produced was the rattling of jewelry. On this night, however, the fans seemed intent on refuting any allegations of their passivity. They were in it early and often, pleading Deee-feense even as the Bulls opened a lead. And as the Jazz gathered in their huddle during a timeout with a couple of minutes left in the first period, the crowd hammered them with noise, making it

Malone was the power in Utah's frontcourt.

abundantly clear just how big a chance Utah had missed in Game 1.

The Jazz dug in and made a run in the second period, bringing it to 31-29 with a Malone bucket. Just when it seemed Utah might find some life, the killer emerged in Jordan. He drove the Bulls on a tare to a 47-31 lead, scoring and drawing fouls like only he could. At every trip to the free throw line, the fans greeted Jordan with lusty chants of MVP! MVP!

The third period brought only more frustration for Utah. The Bulls' defensive strategy continued to force Stockton to the baseline, continued to make even the simple things difficult. When Kukoc hit a trey midway through the period, Chicago had forged ahead 60-40. Yet Jordan was far from through. The Jazz managed to knock the ball away from him in the lane with four minutes left in the third and his team up by 21, and while his teammates headed upcourt to play defense, Jordan dived into the scrum on the floor to get a piece of a loose ball and force a jump.

Now it was time to show off (sometimes you wonder if Jordan even knows he's doing it). He took a feed from Kukoc on the high right post, quickly circled the defense hard right along the baseline, intent like some shark moving in for the kill, then knifed in at the appropriate moment to cut through an opening for one of his eye-popping reverses, one of those Jordan gymnastic feats with a 9.5 degree of difficulty. Before the fans had even settled back into their seats from cheering, he followed it up with a deep two that pushed the lead to 70-48.

How big was his hunger? That seemed to be the only question. He brought the ball up floor moments later and paused in the middle of his dribble with his arms thrown wide, calling for a spread floor. He had 30 points already, and he wanted more, twisting the Jazz humiliation to the unbearable level.

Jordan finished the night with 38 points, 13 rebounds and nine assists. He would have registered a triple-double if Pippen hadn't blown a late layup, costing him the 10th assist. No matter, the

Bulls coasted to a 2-0 series lead, 97-85.

Sloan's disappointment at his team's performance was deep, and he told his team that immediately after the game. "I was a little upset," he said later. "I wanted them to realize it was disappointing. It should have been disappointing. Because they had never been there before (in the Finals), and I have never been here. At least you owe it to yourself to be able to walk off the floor and say, 'Well I was here, and I put everything I had into it.' Basketball should be that way."

Then he went to the press room and told the media, "I thought we were intimidated right from the beginning of the game. If you allow them to destroy your will to win, it's hard to compete... I didn't think we put all our energy into competing tonight."

The most amazing sight of the evening was John Stockton's face in the postgame press conference. It was screwed, virtually twisted, into a pale mask, as if he so much as twitched it would explode into an unstoppable outbreak of fury. It was a mask that said, "I've missed four games in 13 years and after all those nights of tearing my heart out, I've finally gotten to the show and we're not competing."

I'd seen that ghastly mask on one other face in my life. That was a few years back when I interviewed Jerry West about his Los Angeles Lakers' failings in the 1969 NBA Finals.

"I didn't think it was fair," West said, his face tightening into a scowl, "that you could give so much and maybe play until there was nothing left in your body to give, and you couldn't win. I don't think people really understand the trauma associated with losing. I don't think people realize how miserable you can be, and me in particular. It was terrible. It got to the point with me that I wanted to quit basketball. It was like a slap in the face, like, 'We're not gonna let you win. We don't care how well you play.' I always thought it was personal."

The worst thing about this kind of scowl, of course, is that it scars for life, like some sort of basketball acne. Years from now, somebody will ask Stockton about the 1997 NBA Finals, and that scowl will appear. Pale. Ugly. Twisted. Frightening.

"He gets upset," Sloan would say later when asked about his point guard. "He's been upset a lot of times. Even at me. That's when I don't like to see his face screwed up. He gets upset sometimes. But you know what? When he gets upset, we've always talked about it. 'Cause he cares about winning. He doesn't let it stick with him and harbor ill feelings toward us and toward his teammates."

The Jazz, the team that led the league in field-goal percentage, had shot just 40 percent from the floor and scored just 11 points in the second period, tying the Bulls' own NBA Finals record low set in Game 4 of the 1996 series against Seattle.

Around the press room, and in the stands, people were complaining that the Finals was headed toward a sweep, because the Bulls have a way of dissecting proud opponents. But Stockton's face said the series was headed to Utah, where he would get his team a win, or die trying. That night, as the team plane headed home, Stockton walked back to where the coaches sat to discuss his concerns. He found Sloan already sound asleep.

"He talked to my assistant coach," Sloan would reveal later. "I was asleep. That's a fact. He came back to talk to me, and I was asleep. So he knew he had to talk to one of us."

The chore awaiting the Jazz coaches the next day was watching the unseemly film of Game 2. "That was one I didn't want to have to look at," Sloan said, "but we did."

It left the coach realizing that he probably should have started his team in the motion offense in Game 2, just to throw the Bulls' defense off. It was a ploy Sloan occasionally used with his team. "I probably made a mistake in the second game in Chicago," he said. "I felt like I did. I think sometimes players and teams you're playing against really get zeroed in on knocking you out of the box. We didn't get a very good feeling about ourselves in Game 2 when they came out and defensed us and put us in the nickel seats

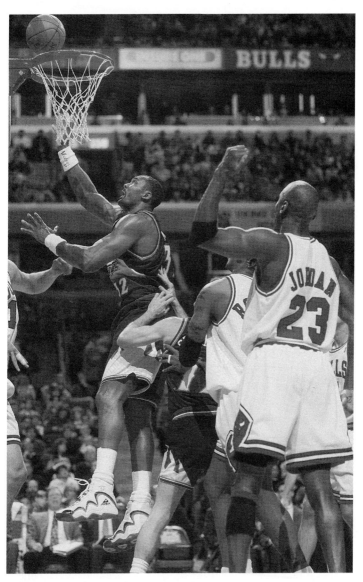

Malone could be overpowering at times.

to start with. We never did get out of it."

Right before Game 3 he told his players to open with their motion offense. "We just decided we try it," he explained later, "to see if we could get a little better feeling about ourselves to start the game."

Sure enough, the motion worked. The Bulls were obviously bothered by the 4,000-foot altitude in Salt Lake City, and remained winded for the better part of a week. The Chicago team had elected to stay in the nearby ski resort of Park City, which had an elevation of about 8,000, in hopes it would help the players adjust for gametime on Friday, June 6. But the Jazz took a 61-46 halftime lead and did a little coasting of their own, pulling the series to 2-1 with a 104-93 victory, during which Jazz fans showered Malone with MVP chants of their own. He answered their support by scoring 37 points with 10 rebounds to lead the rout.

The victory set off a wild celebration in the normally quiet streets of Salt Lake City, much like one would see in the aftermath of an NCAA Final Four. How charged was quiet little Utah for the championship series? An estimated 25,000 people who didn't have tickets gathered outside the arena to watch the game on a giant TV screen.

The tone for the Friday night contest had been set early with the unleashing of an introduction and prolonged applause perhaps unlike anything seen before in championship series history. A dozen giant bags dumped an avalanche of aqua, gold, white and purple balloons from the rafters in conjunction with a battery of fireworks blasting away at center court, the result of which made the place sound an awful lot like Beirut, a sensation drawn out over the next several minutes as the fans popped thousands of balloons, like the crackling of small arms fire. At the height of the spectacle, the Jazz mascot rolled a full-throated Harley Davidson motorcycle onto the floor, revving and rumbling and smoking in defiance.

The whole display was way over the top, Phil Jackson later told

Stockton's competitiveness was a huge factor in the Jazz comeback.

Russell and Malone worked the boards.

reporters, an opinion the Bulls' coaching staff reinforced by inserting earplugs for the introductions of the next two games.

Yet noise was a minor concern alongside the Bulls' struggling offense. They had managed to scare the Jazz with a 16-3 run in the second half, driven by Jordan's and Pippen's three-point shooting (Pippen even tied an NBA Finals record with seven treys). But the Jazz had found success by bumping Chicago's shooters in the low post and forcing the Bulls to take perimeter shots. The result was the opening of a crease in Chicago's confidence.

To make sure the Bulls didn't get too comfortable for Sunday's Game 4, a local radio station began attempting early wake-up calls at their quarters, and someone went to the extra effort of having a band strike up an early-morning tune outside the visitors' quarters in Park City, all in response to a similar ploy aimed at the Jazz by a radio station in Chicago earlier in the series.

Chicago's Dennis Rodman then added his goofy contribution to the distractions. Asked during a Saturday media session about his lackluster play the night before, he attempted to make light of it with a quip blaming everything on Utah's largely Mormon population, whom he described with an expletive. Although the throng of reporters gathered round him laughed loudly at his comment, it was a terrible choice of words, one that netted him a record $50,000 fine from the league.

Rodman and his teammates were greeted by the din of Utah's Delta Center for Game 4 on Sunday, June 8. As introductions were set to begin, Bulls equipment manager Johnny Ligmanowski strolled across midcourt waving broadly to a friend among the frenzied Utah crowd. There certainly weren't many Bulls friends in the building. That became apparent with the tumult that arose as the pregame clock wound down.

Encouraged by Jackson's complaints, Utah's fans and game operations staff were ready with another round of exploding fireworks and thunderous applause, highlighted by some furry creature rapelling out of the rafters with spinning sparklers exploding on this head. Fortunately, the only motorcyle on the premises this time was Malone's, and it was parked in a storage area.

Regardless, the afternoon unfolded as what was easily the Bulls' biggest disappointment of the season. Their offense still sputtered, but their defense for 45 minutes was spectacular. With 2:38 to go in the game, the Bulls had willed their way to a 71-66 lead and seemed set to control the series 3-1. But that's when Stockton immediately reversed the momentum with a 25-foot three-pointer.

Jordan came right back with a 16-foot trey, and when Hornacek missed a runner, the Bulls had a chance to close it out. Instead, Stockton timed a steal from Jordan at the top of the key and drove the length of the court. In a move that awed Sloan, Jordan recovered, raced downcourt and managed to block the shot, only to get whistled for a body foul, a call that might not have been made in Chicago, Jordan later suggested.

Stockton made one of two free throws to pull Utah within three. Pippen then missed a corner jumper, Stockton was fouled and made both with 1:03 left, to cut the lead back to 73-72. Jordan missed a jumper on the next possession, Stockton rebounded and looped a perfect baseball pass down to Malone for a 74-73 Utah lead.

"If you could have suspended time while the ball was in the air, Jerry would have strangled me," Stockton said of Sloan's courtside agony.

The Bulls' next possession brought a wide-open Steve Kerr three-pointer attempt from the right corner that missed. With 17 seconds left, Chicago fouled Malone, setting up repeat circumstances from Game 1. Would he miss again in the clutch? Pippen wanted to talk to him about that, but Hornacek stepped in to keep him away from the Mailman.

"I knew what he was doing, trying to talk to me," Malone said. "He still talked to me the whole time I was shooting."

Pippen went into rebounding position and yelled "Karl!, Karl!"

"Usually I think about faraway places, but this time I thought about 650 million people watching all over the world," Malone said. "I won't lie to you. That's what I thought about the whole time."

His first shot knocked around the rim before falling in, smoothing the way for the second and a 76-73 lead. With no timeouts, the Bulls were left with only a rushed three-point miss by Jordan, which Utah punctuated with a breakaway slam for the 78-73 final, the second lowest scoring game in league championship history.

"I guess the Mailman delivers on Sundays out here," Pippen acknowledged afterward.

"We were flat," Tex Winter said. "We simply did not react. Even our quick reactors. Michael was a slow reactor. He looked like he was running in a plowed field."

Jordan had scored 22 points, and a foreign journalist, from among the 1,000 media representatives worldwide granted credentials to cover the series, asked him if he felt mortal.

"There's gonna be games where I can't live up to the fantasy or the hype of what people have built up Michael Jordan to be," he replied. "I'm accustomed to living with that."

END GAME

After moving at a breakneck pace, playing every other day, the NBA Finals slowed down, giving both teams an agonizing three-day wait before pivotal Game 5 on Wednesday. Asked about the time off, Chicago's Jud Buechler said, "To be honest, it's a lot of nerves. We've been sitting around. We've lost two in a row. The last loss obviously really took a lot out of us. I thought we controlled the game except for the last minute and 45 seconds. Sitting around in Park City, thinking about the loss, thinking about what I coulda done, what the team coulda done, that's tough. It's hard to relieve that tension. Our families are here, which has been nice.

You try to do something with them to get your mind off it; you see a movie or something, but you just have flashbacks of the game. It's on your mind the whole time."

Actually none of the Bulls seemed too relaxed. Kukoc was shooting 34 percent for the series and averaging 7.5 points. Steve Kerr had made only three of his 12 trey attempts. Harper was shooting 33 percent and averaging 5.5 points. Rodman was averaging a little over five rebounds in each of the first four games. Even Jordan, who had shot 51 percent in the first two games, had seen his shooting drop to 40 percent in the next two.

"They're giving us everything we can ask for," Pippen said of the Jazz. "Five, six days ago, everyone was predicting that we would sweep this team. Now everything is turned around. It's been very difficult for us. It's more difficult for us than any team we've faced in the finals."

The anxiety was hanging over the Bulls like the thunderstorms that rolled up Utah's cottonwood canyons as Game 5 approached. Just when it seemed their predicament couldn't get worse, Jordan was hit with a viral illness in the wee hours before Wednesday's game. The first shock of the news hit his teammates at the morning pregame shootaround. He was too sick to attend. Jordan miss a practice? Never.

The stillness that settled over the team in the hours before Game 5 unsettled second-year forward Jason Caffey. "It's kinda scary," he said, sitting wide-eyed in the locker room before the game.

In the darkness of the training room a few feet away, Jordan lay like some sick puppy. However, some veteran Bulls observers weren't fooled. "Michael's sick?" one asked. "He'll score 40."

Actually the total came to 38, including the back-breaking three down the stretch to deliver the Bulls from the dizzying altitude. Despite his well-known flair for the dramatic, this perfor-mance was no act. "I've played a lot of seasons with Michael and I've never seen him so sick," Pippen said afterward. "I didn't know

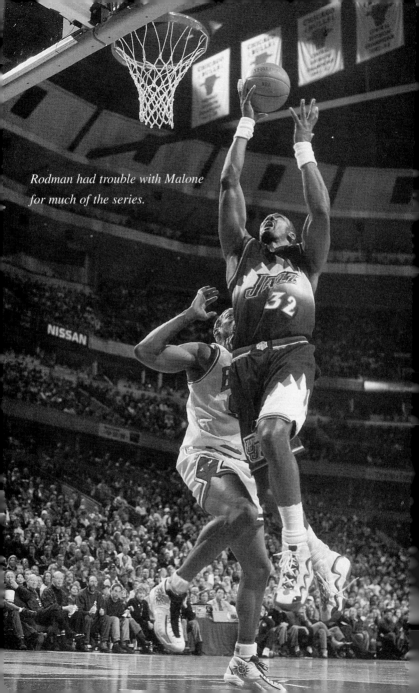

Rodman had trouble with Malone for much of the series.

if he would even put his uniform on. He's the greatest, and definitely the MVP in my mind."

The Jazz came out strong, riding on the emotion of their crowd and the confidence of their 23-game home winning streak. Jordan scored Chicago's first four points, then faltered weakly while Utah rushed out to a 16-point lead early in the second quarter, 34-18, on an Antoine Carr jumper.

Jordan, though, fixed his focus on the rim and started taking the ball inside. He contributed six points on a 19-6 Chicago run that pulled the Bulls to 42-39. Malone, meanwhile, was forced to sit with an early third foul. Jordan's inside work also produced eight free throws in the quarter and helped give Chicago its first lead, 45-44. Malone again found more foul trouble in the third as the pace slowed, but Utah forged a five-point lead to start the fourth and expanded it to eight early in the quarter.

Unfortunately, it was Michael Time. He scored 15 points down the stretch to shove the pressure right at the Jazz. The Bulls were down by one when he went to the free throw line with 46 seconds to go. He hit the first, but snatched up the loose ball when he missed the second. Moments later he hit a three on a pass from Pippen, pushing the Bulls to an 88-85 lead.

Utah's Greg Ostertag scored on a dunk to cut Chicago's lead to 88-87 with 15 seconds left, but on the ensuing inbounds play Pippen dribbled into the open court and found Longley underneath for a slam. Up 90-87, the Bulls relied on their defense to force Hornacek into an off-balance three pointer. The Jazz controlled the miss, and Stockton made a final free throw. But the Bulls had ridden their championship experience to a decisive 3-2 series lead. Jordan stood under the Utah basket jutting his fists into the air triumphantly as the game ended.

"As far as big wins, I think this is as big a win as we've had in a playoff situation like this, especially getting down in the first half and having fought back," Phil Jackson said.

"I almost played myself into passing out," Jordan said. "I came in and I was dehydrated, and it was all to win a basketball game. I gave a lot of effort, and I'm just glad we won because it would have been devastating if we had lost."

"The victory here ranks among the top we've had," Pippen said. "To come in and beat a very good basketball team on their home floor, where they could have put our backs to the wall, we showed what champions can do."

The Jazz valiantly took the lead early in Game 6 back in Chicago and kept it until the Bulls' pressure finally ate it away down the stretch, with Jordan driving the issue just enough to allow Chicago to claim the series on yet another last-second shot, this time by Steve Kerr. The Jazz had scratched and clawed but lost narrowly, leaving Chicago's players and management to avow that they'd never faced such a fight in their four previous championship bouts.

In the Bulls' locker room after the game, Jazz owner Larry Miller offered his congratulations. The experience of reaching the NBA Finals had been gigantic for his team, he said. "It blows my mind how professional things have been with the league and both arenas, just the sheer weight of the exposure, the media exposure, the fan involvement in both cities, it's just incredible. We thought we'd always had vocal fans before, but it's got a whole new level this year. There's been a lot made about the Chicago fans being quiet. If they were, they overcame it tonight. I feel good about it. We stayed in there in every game. I can handle losing if we don't cave in and give it to them. I don't like losing. But we stood our ground and played hard tonight. We put everything we had on the floor tonight. Not a thing was left in the locker room."

Certainly Stockton and Malone hadn't left anything back.

Asked about the plays made by his 6-1 point guard, Sloan said, "As small as he is, I don't think anybody realizes how big his hands are, and he has a will to want to win. He's not overpowering with his body, but he has a tremendous will to want to win."

People have compared Stockton with Celtic great Bob Cousy,

Jazz backup point guard Howard Eisley had an excellent finals series.

but that's inaccurate. Cousy was a fancy dancer. The next fancy thing John Stockton does will be his first. Stockton is much more like Jerry West. He has an anger for winning.

Malone is the same way. He was so nauseated by the outcome that, like West, he talked of quitting. Instead, he went back to work, which was where the Denver Nuggets coaches found him on that early Sunday morning just days after the championship series ended.

The loss hurt all summer, but Malone had time to think about it. "It has changed some stuff for me," he would say later of the experience he gained fighting the Bulls for the title. "I'm looking forward to getting back there again and representing the Jazz. It's a tremendous amount of confidence we have. If we get back there, we know we can win it."

Malone had been frustrated when training camp for the 1997-98 season opened and some of the team's younger players came back in less than top shape. Coupled with Stockton's injury, the circumstances left the Jazz struggling until Stockton returned in December. "It was frustrating because guys should have come back raring to go," Malone said at the 1998 All Star Game in New York. "But we're starting to get there now."

Indeed, as spring returned to the NBA, the Jazz were on another winning streak, attempting to push Seattle and Chicago for the best record in the league. The one constant in the whole season, Malone said, was Jerry Sloan's competitiveness. "I love it," the power forward said. "It's greater now than it ever has been, and I love it. Just being Jerry Sloan. He's more competitive than he's ever been."

It's the attitude that defines the Utah Jazz, an attitude that sums up the way basketball things ought to be. Competing. Uncompromising. Laying your heart on the line each and every night and being unafraid of the consequences. Then getting up the next day and starting all over again.